FEBRUARY 2017

Every Dog's Dream Rescue

A portion of all profits earned from your purchase of this book will be sent to Every Dog's Dream Rescue, Inc., a group of compassionate volunteers working around the clock to provide a safe haven for all the animals that are bought into their rescue facility. Every Dog's Dream not only maintains high-quality care for rescued dogs; they also take in cats and small animals. They operate an adoption center located within the Petco facility on Harry L. Drive in Johnson City, New York, where they always have an abundance of cats and kittens and a number of puppies up for adoption. Every Dog's Dream helps families across New York State to care for stray cats. They also help provide food and veterinary care for those who cannot afford to pay but don't want to give up their animals.

To find out more or to donate, go to: EveryDogsDream.org

Caring for Small Animals

Village Earth Press

Village Earth Press
Vestal, New York 13850
www.villageearthpress.com

First Printing
9 8 7 6 5 4 3 2 1

ISBN: 978-1-62524-452-9
series ISBN: 978-1-62524-449-9

Author: Rae Simons
Design: Micaela Grace Sanna

Caring for Small Animals

RAE SIMONS

VILLAGE EARTH PRESS

TABLE OF CONTENTS:

Did You Know?

The hedgehog got its name because wild hedgehogs like to live in hedges, where they can find insects, worms, and frogs to eat.

Introduction

To parents and teachers:

. . . .

Animal lives matter. Human welfare and animal welfare are interwoven so tightly that they cannot be separated. In other words, what hurts animals will ultimately hurt us as well.

We can see this at the planetary level. As animals lose their habitats because of climate change, pollution, deforestation, and other factors, human well-being is also threatened. Sometimes, people seem to think it's an either-or situation: we either help people (by investing in businesses that are harming the environment) or we help animals (by hindering the success of those same businesses). That's not the way things work on our planet, though. We are all in this together. What puts animals at risk is an equal risk to human well-being.

We are not only linked to animals at the biological and environmental level. We also share many of the same emotions with them—and how we treat animals can't be separated from how we treat each other. Mark Bekoff, an evolutionary biologist, said in an interview with *Forbes* magazine:

> how we treat other animals has direct effects on how we feel about ourselves …compassion begets compassion…. So, when we're nice to other animals and empathize compassionately with their physical and mental health we're also spreading compassion to other people.

The more scientists learn about animals, the more they find that the creatures with whom we share our planet are far more amazing than we ever knew. Scientists have proven that even fish are conscious and sentient; they've discovered that it's not only our dogs who are sensitive to our pain but that rats, mice, and even chickens are as well; and they also have proof that crows can use tools that are more sophisticated than chimpanzees'. What's more, based on animals' neurochemicals, our furred and feathered friends experience the same feelings of love that humans do.

Earlier cultures thought of animals as our brothers and sisters, but somehow, our culture lost track of that perspective. We need to regain it, not only for animals' sakes but for our own—and we need to teach it to our children. By teaching children how to care for animals (whether pets, farm animals, or wild animals), we are empowering children to become kinder and more responsible.

Psychologists, educators, and other experts agree. The National PTA Congress wrote:

Children trained to extend justice, kindness, and mercy to animals become more just, kind, and considerate in their relations to each other. Character training along these lines will result in men and women of broader sympathies; more humane, more law abiding, in every respect more valuable citizens.

When children learn compassion and respect for animals, they are better able to extend compassion and respect to each other. A relationship with an animal also helps children gain self-confidence; research even indicates that being with an animal helps children relax and learn better. And by speaking out for those who cannot speak for themselves, children learn leadership and the power of their own voices to make the world a better place.

Village Earth Press has created this series of books because we believe that we need to take action on animals' behalf. We also believe that children should have opportunities to become all they can be. Our hope is that this book will contribute to both those goals.

Read more on this topic (and then discuss with children what you learn). We recommend these books:

The Emotional Lives of Animals
by Mark Bekoff

The Ten Trusts: What We Must Do to Care for the Animals We Love
by Jane Goodall

The Pig Who Sang to the Moon: The Emotional World of Farm Animals
by Jeffrey Moussaieff Masson

The Bond: Our Kinship with Animals, Our Call to Defend Them
by Wayne Pacelle

chapter 1

The History of Our Smallest Friends

What do you do for fun? You probably watch television a lot. You play games on your computer. Hopefully, you also find some time to run around and play games outside with your friends. Maybe you read books and listen to music. And maybe you have a pet you like to play with.

Now imagine you lived a thousand years ago. You wouldn't have a television or a computer. There would be no iPod or iPad, no smartphone, no CD player. You wouldn't be able to even imagine these things! Your family probably wouldn't have any books either, and if they did, the books weren't for kids. Only a few grown-ups could even read.

So what would you have done for fun if you had been alive back then? Well, you would have still played games with your friends. You would have probably played hide-and-seek, and all kinds of games that used a ball. Your family and friends might have made music together sometimes, and that would have been fun. And maybe you would have had a pet of some sort! You might have had a dog or cat— or maybe a bird, a fish, or even an insect for a pet.

Even longer ago, though, no one had any pets. People were mostly worried about staying alive. They knew animals were important, and they honored them—but people were too busy hunting and gathering food to have time to be friends with animals. Dogs were pretty much the only animals that became friends with humans during this time.

Then humans settled down and began farming. Now they no longer moved around all the time, hunting and

gathering. Their lives changed. Because they now had homes that stayed in one place, they had time to make friends with more animals—like cats. After a while, they also began keeping other animals in their homes too.

Bug Pets

Thousands of years ago, people in Asia kept crickets in cages to warn them of danger in the night. Crickets sing all night, but they get quiet if they hear a noise. If someone broke into a home, the people inside would know because the crickets would stop singing. Today, people in Japan and other places of the world still keep pet crickets in cages. They like the chirping noise crickets make.

"sing," like crickets and katydids. Now people could enjoy watching these little animals. They thought watching them was as much fun as we think television is today!

About 4,500 years ago, people in ancient Egypt and other nearby lands kept fish in tanks. They considered these fish to be holy. About a thousand years later, the Chinese kept pet fish that were a lot like today's goldfish. The Chinese liked these pet fish because they were pretty. No one was allowed to eat them! Then, about 2,500 years ago,

Many times people kept these animals mostly because they were pretty. People liked looking at them, so they kept birds in cages, and they put fish into tanks. They also kept insects in cages, especially insects that

Pet Fish

The first fish that lived in bowls and tanks didn't live very long. People didn't understand that fish need to "breathe" oxygen from water. If fish use up all the oxygen in the water, they die. In 1805, someone finally learned that fish stayed alive longer if their water was changed often. Then, in 1850, someone else discovered that if you put plants in a fish tank, fish stay alive even longer. This is because the plants make oxygen in the water.

the ancient Romans—people who lived in what is today Italy—kept fish in small ponds. Some Romans liked their pet fish so much that they cried when one died!

The ancient Romans were also some of the first people to keep birds as pets. They kept parrots, because they were so pretty. What the Romans liked best, though, was any bird that could learn to talk. Birds can't really talk, of course, not the way people can—but some birds like to **mimic** the sounds they hear. They can learn to repeat human words.

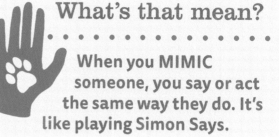

What's that mean?

When you **MIMIC** someone, you say or act the same way they do. It's like playing Simon Says.

The Romans also kept crows, magpies, and starlings as pets. These birds can learn to repeat words the way a parrot can. In ancient Rome, wealthy families enjoyed their pet birds so much that they usually had a slave

Mockingbirds were once popular pets. They mimic the sounds they hear, so they can be taught to repeat songs and words.

Did You Know?

Ancient Romans kept mockingbirds in cages by their front doors to be like doorbells. The birds made noise whenever someone came to the door.

What's that mean?

RODENTS are a type of small animal. They have big front teeth for gnawing on things. Rats, mice, squirrels, chinchillas, guinea pigs, chipmunks, and hamsters are all kinds of rodents. There are more rodents on Earth than there are any other kind of furry animal.

When people BREED a certain kind of animal, they pick which father and mother animals will have babies together. People choose parents that look a certain way, so that their babies will look like that too. By breeding animals, people have created all sorts of funny-looking animals that would never have existed in nature.

The biggest rodent is the capybara.

whose only job was to take care of the birds and teach them to talk! Even poor families often kept songbirds in cages. They enjoyed hearing the birds sing.

About 400 years ago, humans started keeping other small animals as pets. The first pet tortoise belonged to a church leader in London, England. About the same time, explorers to South America brought back guinea pigs to Europe. In South America, people had kept guinea pigs both for food and as pets, but in Europe, no one would have

dreamed of eating a guinea pig. People even had graveyards where they buried their pet guinea pigs when they died!

Before guinea pigs came along, most people considered small animals, especially rodents, to be pests—not pets! Mice and rats got in people's food. These animals also spread diseases. People didn't want to be friends with them. Instead, they kept cats to get rid of small animals like these.

Then, about 200 years ago, people in Japan began to keep mice as pets. The Japanese liked to see all the fancy colors that mice could be. Over the next hundred years, pet mice spread around the world. People enjoyed watching these little animals in their cages. About the same time, people also began to breed pet rats and rabbits. Then, not quite a hundred years ago, hamsters made their way into the pet world. About 50 years ago, gerbils became pets for the first time. After than, pet stores began selling many kinds of small animals as pets.

Did You Know?

Chinchillas were first hunted for their soft fur. It took about 120 chinchillas to make a fur coat. Today, most of the chinchillas in the world are pets.

Hamsters

Hamsters were once wild animals that lived in many parts of the world. Then, in the 1930s, a scientist found some baby hamsters in a field. He took them home and raised them. Like many small furry animals, hamsters have lots of babies—and then their babies have lots of babies. The scientist ended up with LOTS of hamsters. He sent some of them to other scientists to be used in experiments. Finally, some of the hamsters became pets. They were gentle and friendly, and people liked them. Soon, hamsters became one of the small pets people liked best.

Timeline of Small Pets

3000 BCE
People in what is now Brazil keep macaws as pets.

2500 BCE
People in ancient Egypt keep fish in tanks.

1500 BCE
The Chinese keep pretty fish as pets.

100 BCE
The ancient Romans keep fish in small ponds.

50 BCE
People in India think that mynah birds are holy and keep them in special cages.

900s
The Chinese begin to breed different kinds of goldfish.

1000s
Pueblo people in what is today the American Southwest keep macaws in pens.

1369

The emperor of China builds a factory to make tubs for keeping fish.

The shape of the modern goldfish bowl looks just like these tubs.

1493

Christopher Columbus brings Queen Isabella of Spain a pair of parrots from South America.

1652

The first pet tortoise is kept in England.

1768

The governor of the Virginia colony keeps 28 red birds (probably cardinals) in cages.

1828

The first snakes—a type of python—are kept as pets.

1888

The first pet rabbit comes to the United States from England.

1923

The first chinchilla is brought to the United States.

1938

The first hamsters are brought to the United States.

1964
The first gerbils become pets.

1978
The movie *Watership Down* makes rabbits a more popular pet for children.

1990
The first *Teenage Mutant Ninja Turtles* movie makes kids more interested in keeping turtles as pets.

21st century
Pet stores are full of all sorts of small animals—including spiders!

Did You Know?

Scientists use small animals like mice, rats, hamsters, and rabbits for experiments. Small animals are enough like humans that scientists can study them to learn more about diseases and new medicines.

The Inca people in Peru domesticated guinea pigs 3,000 years ago. The Inca ate guinea pigs, but they also kept them as pets sometimes. Guinea pigs didn't become pets in the rest of the world until the 1700s.

Sometimes people call these small animals "pocket pets." People think of them as being so small they can fit in a pocket! Because these animals can live in small spaces, people often think they're also easy to keep. If a family isn't ready for a dog or cat, they may think that a small animal is a better choice.

It's true that a hamster, a fish, a snake, or a tarantula won't need as much space as a dog or cat would. But little animals do need lots of care. You can't just stick them in a cage and forget about them. To do that would be very mean. The animal would

be unhappy and sick. Before long it would die.

If you plan on getting a small pet, you'll need to learn lots of things first. You need to learn what kind of care the animal needs. You need to be sure you have the time and money to spend on taking good care of the animal.

Little pets depend on you to take good care of them. They can't get their own food and water. They can't make their home safer or more comfortable. They have to just sit in their cages waiting for you to do those things. They will die if you don't take care of them. They need YOU!

chapter 2

Fish Tank Friends

Fish come in all shapes and colors. They're pretty to look at and fun to watch. And they're probably the easiest of all pets to care for. But there are still plenty of things you need to know before you get your first fish. And once you have your fish, there are lots of things you'll need to do for him. You can't let yourself ever forget about him. He needs you.

Before you get your fish, you'll need to have a home for him to live in. Talk to the grown-ups in your house about this part. **Aquariums** come in different sizes. The bigger the tank, the more money it will cost—and the more work it will be to keep it clean. You also need to think about how much space you have in your home. A big aquarium takes up a lot of space!

Next you'll need to decide on a good place to put your aquarium. Fish don't like to have their water too hot or too cold. They also don't like the water to be warm part of the day and then change to cold. This means that you want to be careful about putting your

This kind of bowl isn't good for fish. Goldfish that live in little bowls like this don't have room to grow. They don't have the things they need to be healthy. They die sooner.

aquarium too near a window. It could be cold there sometimes. On sunny days, it could get too warm. That wouldn't be good for your fish. You also don't want to put your fish too near a heater, radiator, or fireplace.

Fish don't like loud sounds either. They'll be happier if they live somewhere that's not right next to the television. They won't like it if you play really loud music around them.

What's that mean?

An AQUARIUM is a special tank for fish. It's a home for pet fish.

You can't just put your new fish in an empty glass tank. Your aquarium should have gravel on the bottom. It should have places for your fish to hide when he wants to. You will need a light and a filter to help keep the tank clean. You can put live plants in the aquarium, but they'll need care as well. The aquarium in this picture is quite large. You could get a smaller tank—but the smaller the tank, the fewer fish you should have.

Last of all, you need to make sure you put your aquarium somewhere it will be safe. If it's a large aquarium, you might need a special stand for it. If it's smaller, it can go on a table or a counter—but make sure it's not somewhere it's going to get bumped or tipped over.

When you have your aquarium all set, it's time to fill it up with water. The water that comes out of your faucet may not be the right water, though. It could have things in it that would hurt or kill your fish. At the pet store, you can buy whatever you need to make your water safe for your new fish. Ask the people there to help you.

Cats love to watch fish. Make sure your fish are safe from furry paws!

ALGAE PAD

HEATER

NET

FILTER

Here are other things you'll need for your fish. The blue sponge is a special pad for wiping off algae. (Algae is the green stuff that grows on fish tanks.) The heater is something you'll need for some fish, but not for others. It keeps the water the right temperature for fish that need to live in warmer water. The net will help you take things out of your tank or move your fish to another tank. The filter takes dirt out of the water, so you won't need to change the water so often.

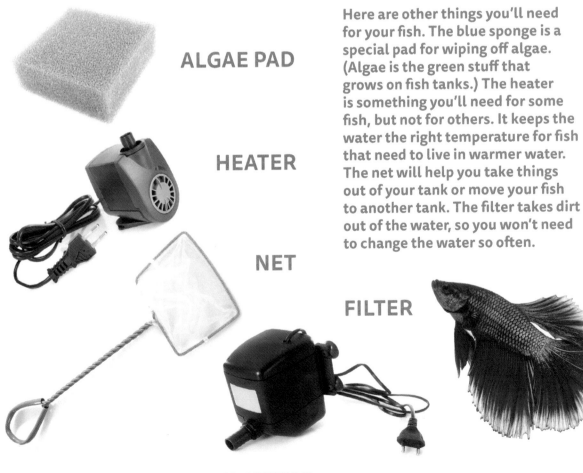

You'll also need food for your fish. You can buy this at the pet store too. Be sure to get the right kind for whatever fish you decide to bring home. Follow the feeding instructions carefully. Never feed your fish too much or too often. He won't be able to eat so much food, and his water will get dirty. That's not good for him.

Finally, you're ready to decide what kind of fish you want. Pet fish can be either saltwater or freshwater. Saltwater fish are often very colorful and pretty—but they're a lot harder to care for. If you get saltwater fish, they'll need a different kind of aquarium. Grown-ups will need to help you take care of it. So you'll probably want to start out with freshwater fish.

Did You Know?

Fish poop. They poop a lot. That's one reason aquariums get dirty. A filter helps to take their poop out of the water.

Here are some different kinds of freshwater fish you might think about getting.

Goldfish

Goldfish are pretty easy to take care of, and they get along with most other fish. They like their water a little cooler, though (about 63 degrees Fahrenheit), so they won't be happy with angel fish, bettas, and mollies. Goldfish make lots of poop, which means you'll need a filter. They also like little places to hide, so put plants or other things where they can feel safe.

Angel Fish

Angel fish are beautiful. Like mollies, they like their water a little warmer, so you'll need a heater. Because of the way they're shaped, they need a deeper, bigger tank than some smaller fish do. If you give them a large tank that holds at least 30 gallons, they'll have room to grow. They could grow to be as big as your hand!

Guppy

These tiny little fish get along with most other fish, but they like to hang out with other guppies, so try to get a few together. They come in different colors, with fancy tails and plain tails. The colorful ones are usually males, while most of the silvery ones are female. Because guppies are so small, don't put them in with bigger fish that might eat them.

Molly Fish

Mollies come in different colors, with and without spots. Mollies get along well with other fish. They need freshwater tanks that are slightly warmer, which means you'll need a heater for their aquarium. They love to hang and hide in plant life, so make sure you have either live plants or plastic plants for them. They do better with a little bit of salt in their water. You can add "aquarium salt" to the water before you put them in—but always check with your pet shop to make sure you add exactly the right amount for them. Also, if you have other fish in the tank, you need to ask someone at the pet store if the salt might hurt those fish.

Betta Fish

Bettas are very beautiful—but you can never put two males in the same tank. If you, do they will fight each other until one of them dies. They don't do well with other fish either, so these fish do better all by themselves. You'll need a cover on your betta fish's aquarium, because he can jump out! He needs a tank that holds at least 2.5 gallons of water. A 5-gallon tank is even better. He likes his water temperature to always be between 75 and 82 degrees Fahrenheit, so you'll need a heater with a thermometer. Don't put sharp things in your tank or plastic plants, because bettas can tear their pretty tails and fins.

Platy Fish

You might think this is a goldfish, but it's not. Platys can be other colors too—red, blue, and black. They swim around a lot, so they're fun to watch. If you have a male and female fish together, be prepared for babies—hundreds of them at a time. That might sound like fun, but babies will need special care. If you're not careful, the grown-up fish will eat them!

Fish need oxygen, just like you do. If you don't have plants in your aquarium to make oxygen for your fish, you can put in a bubbler that will suck oxygen from the air into the tank.

When shopping for your fish, make sure you pick ones that aren't sick. You can tell which ones are healthy by how much they move around. Do they have clear eyes? Can you see any sores on them? You don't want to bring home your new friends and then have them die right away!

Sooner or later, though, all fish do die. They get old, just like people do—but a lot sooner! It's sad when anything dies. You might want to bury your fish and have a funeral for him—but it's okay if you just flush him down the toilet. Do whatever seems best to you.

If you have other fish in the tank, it's important that you use a net to get the dead fish out of the tank right away. If you leave him there, he could make the other fish sick.

There are many more things you can learn about fish. Before you bring a fish home, talk to the people at your pet store and find out exactly what your fish will need. You can also read books and check out websites to find out more. And always remember—your fish needs you to take care of him. If you forget to feed him or take care of his aquarium, he'll die. He's counting on you!

Here are some good books and websites about taking care of fish:

Aquarium Care of Bettas (Animal Planet® Pet Care Library)
by David E. Boruchowitz

Caring for Your Fish
by Kari Schuetz

Choosing a Fish
by Laura S. Jeffrey

How to Take Care of Fish
www.wikihow.com/Take-Care-of-Your-Fish-(Tanks)

Taking Care of Pet Fish
www.kidpointz.com/parenting-articles/elementary-school/social/view/
pet-fish-kids

3 chapter

Creepy-Crawly Pets

Do you think bugs are yucky? Or do you they're cool? Lots of people are scared of crawly things, but they're actually very interesting creatures. If you're thinking about getting your very first pet—or even if you want to add a new member to your creature family—insects and other crawly things can be a good choice.

Unlike any other pet, it's okay to catch an insect outside and bring it home—so long as you take care of it. Insects don't need very much space to be happy and healthy. This means you don't need to spend a whole lot of money on your new pet, the way you might with other animal friends.

These are insects that can live happily in your home.

Crickets

These insects have wing covers with no wings underneath. This means they can't fly—but they CAN hop! People love to hear crickets "sing." They make a chirping noise by rubbing the top of one wing cover along the teeth at the bottom of the other wing. It's a little like playing a violin. Crickets can be kept in a large glass bowl or aquarium. The container should have several inches of soil on the bottom. The top should be covered with a piece of cheesecloth or wire screening, so your crickets have plenty air but can't escape. Give your crickets lettuce, fruit, and moist bread. They will also eat dry dog food.

Praying Mantis

A praying mantis isn't really praying, of course. It just looks like it is because of the way it holds its front legs. In the spring, look for an egg case like the one shown in the picture. Keep an eye on it, and before long, you'll see tiny baby mantises coming out of it. Now you can bring one home. A fish aquarium with a screened top makes a good home for your new pet. Put a layer of soil on the bottom. Make sure your mantis has small plants or small branches to climb on. Don't put more than one adult mantis together, because they'll eat each other. Mantises will eat only live insects, so you'll need to catch flies, moths, or other insects for them. Unlike other animals, praying mantises don't need to eat every day. Give them a meal every 2 to 4 days, and they'll be happy. Make sure your pet actually eats the food—and that it doesn't escape! You don't want your praying mantis to starve to death.

Ant-Lions

You can find ant-lions at the bottom of little cone-shaped pits in sandy soil, like the one in the picture. An ant-lion waits at the bottom of the pit until an ant or other insect comes along and falls in. Then the ant-lion eats it! Sometimes insects don't fall into the pit for weeks, but ant-lions don't need to eat very often. If you find one and bring it home, it needs to live in a shallow box or dish filled with sand. Then you need to make sure to put ants in the box or other tiny crawling creatures. The ant-lions will build pits to catch their food. Some people call ant-lions "doodle-bugs," because they make marks that look like doodles in sand.

Caterpillars

Watching a caterpillar build a cocoon or chrysalis is a lot of fun. It's even more fun when a butterfly comes out! When you find a caterpillar, pay attention to the plants around where you find it. You'll need to give it the same kind of leaves to eat. A large jar makes a good home for a caterpillar, but make sure the lid has holes in it so your new friend can breathe. Put in small branches and leaves from the plant it was eating when you found it. When it's time, the caterpillar makes a hard, shiny case for itself that's called a chrysalis. Some kinds of caterpillars then spin a ball of fuzz around the chrysalis. That's called a cocoon. Now you have to wait. Don't try to open the chrysalis. If you do, the creature inside will die. When the moth or butterfly finally comes out, the wings will be wet and stuck to its body. Don't touch it until the wings dry and unfold. Once the butterfly can fly, you can let it go outside.

Ants

Ants like to live with lots of other ants. They build their own "towns" underground. You can buy something that's called an ant farm at many pet stores. Most of these come with the ants already inside. The ants build their tunnels between two pieces of glass. This means you can watch them as they go about their business. You will see them carry their food to special "rooms" where they'll store it. You'll be able to watch them take care of their eggs and their babies. But don't forget to feed them! Ant farms come with instructions that tell you what your ants need to eat. Most ants like sugar water. They also like fruit and small dead flies.

You can buy some types of creepy-crawly pets in pet stores. One of these is the tarantula. Getting a tarantula is not at all the same thing as finding a bug outside and bringing it home. Taking care of a tarantula is a big **responsibility**. If you buy an adult tarantula, you're getting an animal that could be as old as you are! It deserves to be treated with **respect**. If you take good care of it, it will live for many more years.

A small aquarium makes a good cage for a tarantula. Put potting soil or special pet bark on the bottom of the cage. Don't use dirt from your yard! It could have things in it that might make the tarantula sick. Put something in the cage for the tarantula to climb on, and make sure it has a place to hide. Don't put anything sharp in the cage that could hurt your spider. Keep the cage in a warm place in your house. When tarantulas are in the wild, they only live in the Earth's warm places. Even carrying a tarantula's cage outside for a few minutes in the winter can kill it.

What's that mean?

A RESPONSIBILITY is a job you to do, even when you don't feel like doing it. It's something that others are counting on you to do.

RESPECT means treating people and animals the way you would like to be treated. It means never being mean to them. It means doing your best to understand them.

Tarantulas are a kind of large, furry spider. Like all spiders, they have eight legs.

What's that mean?

When an animal MOLTS, it sheds its old skin or shell. Animals like spiders and crabs have hard outer coverings, instead of a skeleton on the inside the way you do. When you grow, so does your skeleton. But when a spider or crab grows, it needs to get rid of its old hard covering. That's called molting. The creature will get a new, bigger covering. While the new one is growing, though, it's easy for the animal to get hurt or sick.

If you have to move your tarantula when it's cold outside, wrap its cage up in a blanket and keep it covered.

Tarantulas only need to eat once or twice a week. They eat crickets or flies. You can buy these at the pet store, or you can catch them. When your tarantula molts, make sure there are no crickets in the cage, though. The crickets could eat the tarantula. Tarantulas also need water, and you should keep the dirt at the bottom of their cage moist.

Tarantulas are furry, but they don't like to be pet the way you would a cat. They're also easy to hurt. If you drop one, it will probably die. It's a good idea not to handle your tarantula at all. They can't be tamed the way a hamster can. Tarantulas have sharp fangs—and if they feel scared, they could bite you!

There are different kinds of tarantulas. Some types cost more than others. Some kinds move around more. Some are gentler. Some like to dig holes, others like to climb. Another choice is to buy baby tarantulas, called "spiderlings." If you and the grown-ups in your family decide to get a tarantula, talk to the people at a pet store to decide what kind is best for you.

Spiderlings are cheaper than buying an adult tarantula. They need special care, though. If you decide to try to raise baby spiders, you will need to find out exactly what they need to be healthy.

Like all living creatures, tarantulas need food and water.

Hermit crabs are another type of crawly pet. They're a kind of crab that lives inside another sea creature's empty shell. You should buy hermit crabs from a pet store, even though you sometimes see them for sale in beach stores. Don't buy these, because they're often not healthy.

It's cruel to keep a hermit crab without giving it what it really needs. You can't just stick a hermit crab in a jar or a box and expect it to be happy. It needs wet sand at the bottom of its jar, and it like places to hide. Crabs have gills like fish. This mean they get oxygen from water instead of from the air. They need to live in moist places. If the air is too dry, they won't be able to breathe. Without enough moisture around them, they will die.

If you take good care of a hermit crab, it can live 15 to 25 years. Some have even lived to be 40 years old!

A hermit crab also needs fresh water every day. It needs a new bowl of salt water about once a week. Make the salt water by mixing 1.5 teaspoon of salt in one cup of water. Don't use kitchen salt. You can buy special sea salt from a pet

Did You Know?

Hermit crabs can be large or small. One kind of hermit crab can grow to be about as long as your arm—while another kind is only as big as your little toe!

You might be able to find a hermit crab at the beach. It's okay to bring it home with you—but ONLY if you are sure you know how to take care of it and give it a good home!

store. Hermit crabs are easy to feed, because they eat almost anything—raw fish, cooked chicken, cooked beans, cooked peas, cooked corn, nuts, fish food, and fruit. Just don't feed them avocado, because it's poisonous to them. Make sure you keep your hermit crab in a warm place. Also keep some shells in the cage that are larger than the one the crab is using now. When it grows larger, it will need to change shells.

All crawly creatures need care, just like any other animal does. You can't put them in a cage and forget about them. That would be very mean to the small living things that are counting on you to care for them.

If you catch an insect and bring it home, it's okay to let it go if you get tired of it. Just be sure you let it go somewhere it will have what it needs to live and be happy. It's usually best to let it go in the same place where you found it. Don't let it go in the middle of the winter, though, or it may freeze to death.

If you get tired of a tarantula, you can never let it go outside. Instead, you will need to find another home for it. You might want to donate it to a nature center.

If you find a hermit crab at the beach and bring it home, you can take it back and let it go where you found it. If you buy a hermit crab at a pet store, though, you shouldn't let it go at the beach. It may have come from a very different part of the world. It won't be happy to find itself in a strange place. You will need to find it a new home, just like you would any other animal, big or small.

Crawly creatures are interesting to watch. They can be fun pets. They're usually pretty easy to take care of. But don't forget—they need you! If you decide to have one for a pet, it's your job to take care of it.

Here are some good books and a website that will tell you how to take care of crawly pets:

Tarantulas (Animal Planet® Pet Care Library)
by Michael Andreas Jacobi

Fiddler Crabs & Fiddler Crab Care: The Complete Pet Guide
by Alex Halto

Keeping Insects
www.keepinginsects.com

chapter 4

Lizards, Snakes, Frogs —and More!

How would you feel about holding a snake? Do you love to catch a frog in your hands and then let it go? Do lizards and salamanders fascinate you? Do you like to watch turtles sitting in the sun? If you think snakes, lizards, frogs, and turtles are interesting creatures, you might want to think about having one as a pet. **Reptiles** and **amphibians** can make good pets.

If you decide you want a reptile or an amphibian as a pet, get ready to learn a lot before you bring one home! These animals don't usually cost very much, but you will need to buy other things to give your new pet a good home. You should go online and find out more about these creatures. Go to the library and read books about the reptile or amphibian that interests you most. Some of these animals will be easier to take care of than others. Do your **research** before you buy one!

All pets need people to take care of them. If these animals lived in the wild, they could find their own food and make their own houses. But they don't.

Pets live with people, in people's houses. They count on people to give them all the things they need.

Sometimes people get a pet and then decide they've made a mistake. Everyone can make mistakes—but it's never the animal's fault. If you don't want your pet anymore, you are still responsible for it. Sometimes people let their reptiles and amphibians go outside. Animals like these usually came from very different parts of the world, though. They die when they're put in parks or streams where they don't belong. This is a very cruel thing to do. If you can't keep your pet, you need to find someone else who will be responsible for it. You need to make sure it has a good home.

Did You Know?

Salamanders and lizards look kind of alike, but salamanders are amphibians and lizards are reptiles.

What's that mean?

REPTILES are a group of animals that have scales, breathe air, and usually lay eggs. Most reptiles live on land. Alligators, snakes, lizards, and turtles are all reptiles. So were dinosaurs!

AMPHIBIANS live "double lives." They start out as babies that live in water and have gills like fish. As they grow up, they get lungs. Then they leave the water to live mostly on land. They go back to the water to lay their eggs.

When you RESEARCH something, you find out more about it. You find answers to all your questions about that thing. You can do research on a computer online or at a library. You can also do research by asking people questions. Make sure the people you talk to really know the answers you need. Just because someone works at a pet store, doesn't always mean that person knows everything about taking care of animals.

When you are RESPONSIBLE for something, it's your job to take care of it. It's counting on you.

Did You Know?

Turtles and tortoises aren't the same thing. Turtles live in water, and tortoises live on land.

Here are some things you'll need if you have a reptile or an amphibian for a pet:

You'll need an aquarium or cage where the animal will be safe. Large reptiles will need larger cages. Make sure that other pets in the house can't get in and hurt them—and make sure they can't get out! No matter how much you like your snake, you probably don't want to wake up to find her in bed with you.

Because reptiles and amphibians are "cold blooded," they can't keep themselves warm. They need a heater to keep them from getting cold. There are two kinds of heaters. One makes heat that comes down on the animal from the top of its cage. The other kind of heater goes on the bottom of the cage. It makes the sand warm where the animal is sitting.

You'll need dishes for food and water, as well as whatever food your new pet likes to eat. These are mealworms in the picture. Many reptiles and amphibians like to eat them. They also like live crickets and other insects. Large snakes eat mice and other small animals.

Reptiles and amphibians also need sand or something else to put on the bottom of their cages. They needs sticks to climb on and places to hide. Some amphibians may need water for swimming, with rocks where they can climb out and sit.

So how can you tell if a reptile or amphibian might be the right pet for you? Here are some questions to ask yourself:

Am I willing to take care of this animal every day for the rest of its life?

Some reptiles and amphibians live a very long time. Lizards can live 3 to 20 years. Some snakes can live more than 40 years. Turtles and tortoises can live 40 to 100 years or more! That means if you take good care of your pet, it could still be alive when you are a grown-up!

Have I asked the grown-ups in my family if they will help me pay for all the things this pet will need—like a cage, food, and heaters? Will they help me make the kind of home this animal needs?

Taking care of a reptile or an amphibian can be tricky. It also costs money. You need to be sure your family is willing to help you.

Do I have room in my house for a large cage or aquarium?

Even small lizards and frogs will need a space that's large enough for them to move around. Large snakes and lizards may need VERY large cages or tanks.

Can I feed other animals to my pet?

Most reptiles and amphibians eat some kind of live insects or worms. The bigger the reptile, the bigger the animal it eats. Many snakes eat mice, rats, or baby chicks. Will you be okay with that? Or will you feel too sorry for the other animals? In nature, animals eat other animals—but it can be hard to watch in your living room.

You can find many kinds of reptiles at most pet stores. Always make sure the animals look healthy before you buy one. Not all pet stores take good care of their animals. It's always better to adopt an unwanted animal than to buy one at the store.

Have I done my research? Do I really know what my pet will need?

Never bring home any animal until you know exactly what that animal needs to be happy and healthy. Make sure you have its home all ready for it. If you can't give it what it needs, don't bring it home!

Do I know what kind and size of reptile or amphibian would be best for me?

It's a good idea to start out with smaller creatures. Some will be easier to take care of than others. Many of these animals can start out small—and then grow to be BIG. Make sure you know how big your pet will get before you bring it home.

If you're absolutely sure you want a reptile or amphibian, what do you do next? Never catch a reptile from the wild—and if you can, adopt an animal instead of buying it at a pet store. When you adopt a pet, you give a home to an animal whose owners no longer wanted it.

There are special groups of people who rescue animals that have bad homes. People who rescue reptiles and amphibians are sometimes called "herps." That's because "herp" is also another name for reptiles and amphibians. It comes from a word that means "creeping thing." People who are herps love reptiles and amphibians, and they know a whole lot about them. If you go online, you'll probably find that there's a herp group near you. Get in touch with them. They can teach you everything you need to know. They can help you decide whether you're really ready for your pet.

Did You Know?

Geckos have tiny little suction cups on their toes. They use them to crawl up walls. They can even crawl across a ceiling without falling off!

Here are some of the reptiles and amphibians that people keep as pets.

Turtles

You might think turtles would be easy pets, but they need a lot of care—and a lot of space. They start out small, but they grow fairly fast, so they need a large tank. Once they're grown up, they should live in a 75- to 125-gallon tank. They need water to swim in, as well as rocks to sit on. They need a heater, and they also need a special kind of light called ultraviolet. Baby turtles like mealworms, but adult turtles eat mostly vegetables.

Tadpoles

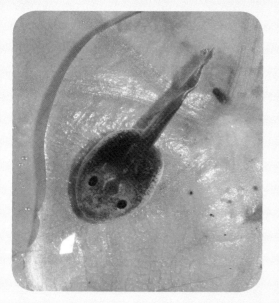

Tadpoles are baby frogs. These are about the only amphibian or reptile that's okay to catch in the wild. You can find them in ponds and sometimes in big puddles. You will need a jar filled with the water where you found the tadpoles. Put water plants in it. Give your tadpoles lettuce and algae to eat. Keep an eye on them because before long they'll start to grow legs. Now they'll need a rock where they can climb out of the water so they can practice breathing. Once they have four legs, it's time to take them back where you found them and let them go.

Iguanas

These guys start out tiny—but they grow more than 12 inches a year for the first several years of their lives. They end up as long as most grown-ups are tall! They also have more than a hundred very sharp teeth. Adult iguanas are dangerous. They look cute when they're babies, but they are NOT good pets.

Bearded Dragons

These creatures look like baby dinosaurs. They make much better pets than iguanas because they're gentle and don't grow too big. They eat both insects and vegetables, and they like to wave their "hands" in the air. They can live to be 10 years old or more.

Chameleons

These reptiles eat live insects. There are different kinds of chameleons. Some of them are very pretty, like this little guy. Most of them live about 3 years. They don't get much bigger than a foot long. There a few types of chameleon, though, that grow to be 2 feet long or more.

Anoles

These small lizards also eat live insects—crickets, moths, flies, and mealworms. They grow to be 6 to 8 inches long, and they usually live about 3 years.

Green Tree Frogs

These small amphibians come from warm parts of the United States, so they'll need a heater under the sand at one end of their home. Sticks and plastic plants will give the frog places to hide and climb. It needs fresh, clean water in a shallow bowl. Use the kind of water you buy at the store, not the water that comes from your faucet, and change it every day. You should also spray your frog and its home every day with the same type of water, using a "mister." Tree frogs eat insects—flies, crickets, and small moths. They also like to "sing." If you take good care of a tree frog, it can live about 5 years.

Ball Pythons

These snakes can make good pets, but you need to know how to take care of them. They don't need to eat very often, but when they do eat, they'll need a dinner of mice, rats, gerbils, or chicks. Baby pythons are about 10 inches long. They grow up to be 5 or 6 feet long, but they don't need as much space as you might think. They do want a box where they can hide, and they will need a heater in their tank or cage. They can live to be 30 years old or more.

Corn Snakes

These snakes also eat little animals. They only need to eat about once every 10 days, though. They grow to be 3 or 4 feet long, and they live about 10 years.

Here are some good books and websites for you and the grown-ups in your family to read before you decide to bring home a reptile or amphibian:

Bearded Dragons (Animal Planet® Pet Care Library)
by Thomas Mazorlig

The New Encyclopedia of Snakes
by Chris Mattison

Animal World: Keeping Reptiles and Amphibians as Pets
http://animal-world.com/encyclo/reptiles/information/reptilecare.php

PETA: Caring for Reptiles
http://www.peta.org/living/companion-animals/caring-animal-companions/caring-reptiles

5 chapter

Feathered Friends

Birds make good pets. Many of them are very smart. They love to learn new things. They can love people just as much as dogs and cats do.

All those are good things—but they also mean that birds need to be around people. You can't just leave them alone in a cage. Imagine how you would feel if someone left you all alone somewhere you couldn't move around freely! You'd feel sad and lonely and bored. Birds feel the same way. They need people to talk to them. They like to have interesting things in their lives. If they don't have those things, they can get sad and sick.

Birds are easier to care for than a dog or a cat. They don't need to go for walks. They don't need to live in a large house or apartment. They don't need to be brushed or washed. Their food doesn't cost much. They don't need to learn to go to the bathroom in a box. You do have to clean out their cage—but that's easier than scooping kitty litter! It's also easier than having to take a dog outside to go to the bathroom. Birds can be messy, though. You'll probably need to sweep the floor around their cage every day.

Did You Know?

Birds need to be let out of their cages every day. They like to fly around and sit on your shoulder. When you are not around, though, you should always put them back in the cage.

Birds can also be noisy. Some birds make a racket that gets annoying. They can scream so loud that your neighbors might get upset! Some kinds of birds love to mimic noises they hear. They might learn to make a sound like a telephone or a washing machine. Some of these birds can also learn to say words. Teaching a bird to talk is a lot of fun—but sometimes a bird learns words you didn't mean to teach him! It could be pretty embarrassing if your bird says a bad word he's heard you say—or if he makes a noise like a burp right in the middle of a special dinner.

Remember that taking care of any pet will always cost some money. You will need to buy a sturdy cage that is the right size for your bird. Your bird will need toys in his cage. He will need water and food bowls—and food. He will also need to go to a veterinarian for checkups or if he gets sick.

If you take good care of them, many birds live a very long time. Some kinds of birds might even live longer than you do!

Many pet birds love to look at themselves in a mirror.

Here are some questions to talk over with your family before you bring home a pet bird.

1. Do you have enough money to buy a bird and then take care of him?

2. Do you have enough time to spend with a bird every day?

3. How do other people in your family feel about having a bird live in the house?

4. Is there room in your house or apartment for a cage?

5. If your family goes away, is there someone who can take care of your pet while you are gone?

6. Do you have other pets that might hurt a bird? It's not usually safe to have a bird if you also have a cat.

7. Are you willing to find out what it takes to keep a bird healthy and happy? There are lots of things you'll have to learn.

8. Will you and your family mind if your bird is noisy? Will your neighbors mind?

9. Do you have young children in your family? Can they be trusted to be gentle with a bird?

10. Does anyone in your house smoke? Birds can't be around cigarette smoke or they will get sick or die. Hairspray or spray detergent in the air could also kill them.

Birds need to go to the doctor too!

Here are some of the most popular bird pets.

Cockatiels

These small parrots love to snuggle and be petted. Some cockatiels learn to talk, but many are better at whistling. They don't mind being handled, but you should always be very gentle!

Pionus Parrots

These parrots aren't as brightly colored as some of the others, but they're sweet little birds. They're calm and not too loud. They can usually learn to say a few words.

Parakeets

Parakeets are small and don't cost a lot—but they are friendly, gentle, and loving. They can learn to talk, although they have tiny little voices. At first, a new parakeet will be shy. If you take the time to win his trust, he will become a good friend who loves you.

Finches

Finches are another small bird that doesn't cost very much. They need big cages, though, because finches need enough room to exercise their wings. They also like to have a friend or two in the cage with them, so plan on getting two or three finches at once. These birds don't like to be handled or pet. They won't need as much attention as some of other kinds of pet birds.

Cockatoos

Cockatoos are friendly and smart. They can learn to say some words, they can learn tricks, and they can also learn to obey commands, the way a dog can. For example, you might be able to teach a cockatoo, "Go to your cage," or, "Be quiet." They are expensive birds, though, and taking care of them can cost a lot of money. They need lots and lots of attention.

Macaws

These large birds are smart and curious. They need plenty of toys to keep them busy, and they want as much attention as they can get. Taking care of them can be a big job. They are good talkers, and they love their people.

Quaker Parrot

These are cheerful little birds that love to make noise. Some of them learn to talk, while others whistle. If you get them when they're young and treat them gently, they can be very loving to people.

Peach-Faced Lovebirds

These are friendly, lively birds. If they grow up with people and get lots of attention, they will love their owners very much. They like to be handled. They even like riding around inside a pocket or perched on a collar. They can usually learn to say a few words, and they're usually not too loud.

Canaries

If you don't have a lot of time to spend with your bird, canaries are a good choice. They are small birds that don't need big cages, and they're happy to be in their cages most of the time. Like finches, these birds don't like to be touched. Male canaries love to sing—but female canaries are quiet. If you are hoping for a singer, make sure you get a boy canary.

Amazon Parrots

These birds are a little bigger and more expensive than many of the other birds on this list. They are among the best talkers, though, and they love to clown around. They can be noisy, and they will need lots of attention and exercise. They are very smart, which means they can get into trouble if you're not watching!

Do you think you're ready to get a bird for a pet? If you are, don't buy one at the pet store. Instead, find a shelter where you can adopt a bird. People often get birds and then decide they don't want them after all. These birds need homes where they can be safe and loved. The people at the shelter can also help you know exactly the right bird for you and your family.

Like all animals, birds should always be treated with care and respect. Birds have small bones, and they must be handled gently. You can't play roughly with a bird. A bird can also hurt you. Many pet birds have large beaks, and they can use them to pinch.

If you and your family decide to get a bird as a pet, you will discover how much fun a bird can be. But never forget—the bird needs YOU. Birds are not toys. You can't play with them and then forget them. Your pet bird will need you to learn all about what he needs to eat and what he likes. He won't be happy or healthy if you don't take good care of him.

Here are some good books and websites for you and the grown-ups in your family to read before you decide to bring home a bird:

ASPCA Pet Care Guide: Birds
by Mark Evans

Kids' Top 10 Pet Birds
by Wendy Mead and Joanna Ponto

Basic Pet Bird Care
www.aav.org/?page=basiccare

Caring for Your Bird
pets.petsmart.com/guides/birds/caring-for-your-bird.shtml

6

Adopting a Small Mammal

Pets like hamsters, gerbils, guinea pigs, and mice are different from other small pets. These furry little creatures are mammals. This means they give birth to live babies. They don't lay eggs like fish, insects, reptiles, and birds do. They live in cages like other small pets, but they need different things to be happy and healthy.

Until quite recently, all rabbits, chinchillas, hedgehogs, and other small furry pets were wild animals. These kinds of animals still live in the wild—but small wild mammals should never be captured and kept as pets. And small mammals who are pets can never be let go into the wild. These pets have never lived on their own in nature. They wouldn't know how to take care of themselves. They would soon die.

Some people think that because these pets are so small that they don't matter as much as larger pets like cats and dogs. Most small furry pets don't cost a lot of money, and that also makes people think they don't matter as much.

That's not true. These little creatures can make wonderful pets—and they need people to take care of them.

Just like with any other kind of pet, you need to think carefully before you decide to get a hamster, rabbit, gerbil, or any other kind of small mammal. You should learn as much as you can about each kind of animal. That way you can decide which one is best for you and your family. Don't just pick the animal you think is cutest! Find out what each animal will need.

If you're getting a small mammal as a pet, you'll need to buy a cage. Make sure it's the right size for the animal. Little animals need room to move around inside their cages. They will need food dishes, water bottles, and toys. They also like things to climb on, such as branches or little ladders. Hamsters, mice, rats, and gerbils like wheels to play on. Running on the wheels helps them get the exercise they need. You can get all the things you'll need at a pet store.

A thousand years ago, people would have thought these little guys were pests! Today, people know that mice make good pets.

Did You Know?

A rodent's teeth never stop growing during its entire lifetime.

Did You Know?

Hamsters are nocturnal. That means they like to be awake at night, and to sleep during the day. This can also mean that your pet hamster might be rattling around in his cage when you're trying to sleep!

Hamsters and other small mammals love to run on a wheel. They also like places to climb and tubes to explore. The more interesting their cage is, the happier they will be.

Once you have a small pet, you need to do everything you can to keep him healthy. Make sure he gets fresh water every day. Give him the right kind of food. Keep his cage clean. He'll need bedding and a house where he can make a nest. Give him fresh bedding once a week and clean out the old bedding. Make sure the bottom of the cage isn't wire, because the wires could hurt his little feet. If you don't do these things, your little animal could get sick. He probably won't live as long.

Even if you're taking good care of your pet, small animals can get sick, just like people do. If your pet has a runny nose or eyes, that could mean he's sick. If the fur is wet or dirty around his tail, that's also a sign that something is wrong. Another sign of sickness is if he no longer wants to run around. If you notice any of these symptoms, you should take your pet to a veterinarian. Not all vets treat small animals, so find one in your area who will BEFORE your pet gets sick. That way if he gets sick, you'll know where to take him right away.

What's that mean?

SYMPTOMS are things that mean you are sick. Coughing or sneezing could be symptoms of a cold. Animals don't usually catch colds, but they have other symptoms that say they are sick.

Little animals enjoy time outside their cages—but you have to be very careful! Because they are so small, they could escape and get lost. Whenever you take a small pet out of the cage, you need to be very sure you have a safe place where he can run around. Keep all electric cords away, so your little friend won't chew on them with his sharp teeth. Make sure no dog or cat will wander by and snap him up.

Most guinea pigs love to be held. If you're holding one and it's wiggling too much, put your hand under her backside. That will make her be still.

One way vets can tell if small animals are sick is by looking in their ears—just like your doctor does with you. If a small animal is sick, a vet can usually give her medicine to make her feel better.

Rats are smart, and they love the people who take care of them. They make good pets.

Did You Know?

When rats are happy or playing, they make a funny sound that sounds like they're laughing.

Here are some of the small mammals that make good pets.

Hamsters

There are different kinds of hamsters. One of the most popular is the Syrian or golden hamster. These little fellows have very short tails. They like to store their food in their cheeks. You should expect a hamster to be sleepy most of the time during the day when you're awake. They can get upset if you bother them when they're sleeping, and they might even bite. They need a wheel in their cage for exercise, along with plenty of things to climb on and crawl through. They like to live alone, so only get one hamster at a time.

Ferrets

Ferrets are quiet, friendly, and curious, but they need more care than many other small mammals. They also cost more. Because they are so smart, they can get in trouble if you don't watch them carefully. They don't need to live in a cage all the time, but you should shut them up when you're not home, so they don't get into mischief. Ferrets in the wild are hunters, so they could eat other small pets. They can usually learn to get along with dog and cats, though. Certain dogs, however, shouldn't be trusted not to hurt a ferret. Ferrets love to play, and they can learn tricks. They can also learn to pee and poop in one place.

Gerbils

Because these little animals come from hot, dry desert lands, they should never go out in the cold. They like to make burrows, so they need enough litter or bedding to dig in. Since they have long tails, make sure their exercise wheels don't have openings where their tails could get caught. They like company, so get either two girls or two boys at the same time. (But don't get one girl and one boy, or you'll end up with more baby gerbils than you want.)

Mice

These little animals are constantly washing and cleaning themselves. They are very FAST, so be careful about letting them out of their cages. Mice do fine alone. If you put two male mice together, they will fight.

Rabbits

Rabbits can be trained to use a box for a toilet, and some people let their rabbits hop around their house without a cage. If you let your rabbit have the run of your house, you have to be very careful that there are no electric cords or anything else dangerous she could chew on. It's a good idea to have a cage as a safe place to put a rabbit when needed. Rabbits get scared very easily. They can even die from fear. A healthy, well-cared-for rabbit, though, can live 7 to 10 years.

Guinea Pigs

No one knows for sure why they're called guinea pigs—they're not pigs, and they didn't come from Guinea! Guinea pigs are very friendly and curious, and they need lots of attention. They like to squeak and squeal. Loud noises make them nervous, though, and they don't like being picked up high in the air. (They do like to be cuddled, though, so long as you're gentle, and they feel safe.) Very hot, very cold, or damp air can be dangerous to them. They need plenty of vitamin C, so make sure they have lots of fruits and vegetables to eat. They have a weird habit of eating vegetables or plants, "pooping" it out in a little pellet, and then eating it again. This isn't as gross as it sounds. These pellets aren't really poop. Guinea pigs just need to eat their food twice to be able to digest it. A guinea pig will live happily with another guinea pig.

Rats

Rats are known for being dirty animals, but that's not true. In fact, they constantly groom themselves with their little paws. They are also very smart. They can learn their names, and they can learn games like peek-a-boo, tug-of-war, and hide-and-seek. Rats are nocturnal, but they can learn to sleep at night like their owners. They have poor eyesight, but they hear and smell very well. Don't use pine shavings or cedar chips as bedding, since these are poisonous for rats. Rats also can't be around cigarette smoke. Never keep just one rat, or he'll be lonely. Always have either two boy rats or two girls rats, so they have company.

Hedgehogs

Hedgehogs are small, but they need a large cage to run around in. They also need some time outside their cage, when they can explore and run around safely. Hedgehogs live alone, so don't get more than one at the same time. Like hamsters, they are nocturnal, so they run around more at night. They live about 4 to 6 years.

Chinchillas

These little animals are more expensive, and they require lots of care. They need a larger cage, with plenty of room. They also need a special kind of sand to "wash" in. (You can buy it at a pet store.) Loud noises and lots of things going on around their cage can make them sick, and very high heat or dampness can kill them. They need things to chew on—but don't let them ever chew on plastic! If they are happy and healthy, they can live from 15 to 22 years.

If you decide that a small mammal is the right pet for you, you could go to a pet store and buy one. Even better, though, you could give a home to an animal that doesn't have one. Rescue shelters that have dogs and cats also often have rabbits, guinea pigs, hamsters, and other small animals. These are animals whose owners didn't want them. Now they need a good home. They need someone to love them.

Little animals have feelings just like you do. They feel tired and hungry. They get scared, and they like to have fun. They need people to give them the things they need to be happy. They need YOU!

Here are some questions to ask yourself before you get any small, furry pet:

1. Have I done my research? Do I know what this animal needs to be happy?

2. Do I have time to take care of this pet?

3. Are there young children in my house who could hurt a small pet without meaning to? Little animals can never be squeezed or treated roughly. They can't be treated like toys.

4. Are there other pets in my house that could be dangerous to a small mammal? Most cats and some dogs won't understand the difference between a wild mouse or bunny and the one that lives in a cage.

5. Do I have enough money to buy a cage, food, and whatever else a small pet needs? If I don't have enough money, will others in my family help me pay for these costs?

6. Do I have a good place to put a cage? Some small pets need larger cages than others. And they all need cages that are in safe places, where they won't feel scared. They also need to live somewhere they won't be too hot or too cold.

Here are some good books and websites for you and the grown-ups in your family to read before you decide to bring home a small mammal:

The Ultimate Encyclopedia of Small Pets & Pet Care
by David Alderton

Looking After Small Pets
by David Alderton

How to Care for Pet Hamsters, Guinea Pigs and Gerbils
parenting.com/article/how-to-care-for-pet-hamsters-guinea-pigs-and-gerbils

How to Care for Gerbils, Hamsters, and Guinea Pigs Report
hellokids.com/c_20670/reading-and-learning/reports-information/animal-information-for-kids/how-to-care-for-gerbils-hamsters-and-guinea-pigs

Image Credits

Cover: Ene (Dreamstime), Jirí Zuzánek, (Dreamstime), Konstantin Sutyagin (Dreamstime), Liumangtiger (Dreamstime), Mav888 (Dreamstime), Photowitch (Dreamstime)

Pages 1–4: Bennymarty (Dreamstime), Brett Critchley (Dreamstime), Cesarz (Shutterstock), Chandru Ganeson (Dreamstime), E. Spek (Dreamstime), Frans Sluijs (Dreamstime), Gvision (Dreamstime), Konstantin Sutyagin (Dreamstime), Kristof Degreef (Dreamstime), Lana Langlois (Dreamstime), Mav888 (Dreamstime), Mgkuijpers (Dreamstime), Micaela Grace Sanna, Onirocosmos (Dreamstime), Paul Murphy (Dreamstime), Roberto Caucino (Dreamstime), Sergey Ryzhov (Shutterstock), Spllogics (Dreamstime), Tom Denham (Dreamstime), Woo Bing Siew (Dreamstime), Xianghong Wu (Dreamstime), Zina Seletskaya (Dreamstime)

Introduction: Photowitch (Dreamstime), Zcello (Dreamstime)

Chapter 1: Andres Rodriguez (Dreamstime), Andygaylor (Dreamstime), Anna Kucherova (Dreamstime), Anna Yakimova (Dreamstime), Charles Brutlag (Dreamstime), David Spates (Dreamstime), Dimitri Surkov (Dreamstime), Eastmanphoto (Dreamstime), Fotoeye75 (Dreamstime), Gulserin Akin (Dreamstime), Irishka777 (Dreamstime), Isselee (Dreamstime), Joanne Zh (Dreamstime), Micaela Grace Sanna, Misad (Dreamstime), Panuruangjan (Dreamstime), Peter Emmett (Dreamstime), Saulichelena (Dreamstime), Swan555 (Dreamstime), Thomas Samantzis (Dreamstime), Tilo (Dreamstime), Vetergor (Dreamstime), Yaroslav Pavlov (Dreamstime), Zhiwei Zhou (Dreamstime)

Chapter 2: Areeya Slangsing (Dreamstime), Basnik,Ben Mcleish (Dreamstime), Carlos Ribet (Dreamstime), Cynoclub (Dreamstime), Dave Bredeson (Dreamstime), Famveldman (Dreamstime), Gavril Margittai (Dreamstime), Micaela Grace Sanna, Narcis Parfenti (Dreamstime), Nikolay Dimitrov (Dreamstime), Tomasz Idczak (Dreamstime), Vonora (Dreamstime)

Chapter 3: Darius Baužys (Dreamstime), Johnbell (Dreamstime), Kavida27 (Dreamstime), Kheki (Dreamstime), Meoita (Dreamstime), Micaela Grace

Sanna, Scott Robinson, Sergey Taran (Dreamstime), Sergio Boccardo (Dreamstime), Sweetcrisis (Dreamstime), Thierry Maffeis (Dreamstime), Vaeenma (Dreamstime), Xtotha (Dreamstime)

Chapter 4: Cathy Keifer (Dreamstime), Cleanylee (Dreamstime), David Watts Jr. (Dreamstime), Dennis Dolkens (Dreamstime), Jean Paul Chassenet (Dreamstime), Lennyfdzz (Dreamstime), Maumyhata (Dreamstime), Micaela Grace Sanna, Mihail Syarov (Dreamstime), Milic Djurovic (Dreamstime), Murdock2013 (Dreamstime), Paulus Rusyanto (Dreamstime), Podius (Dreamstime), Spland06 (Dreamstime), Subin Pumsom (Dreamstime), Svetlana Churkina (Dreamstime)

Chapter 5: Blagov58 (Dreamstime), Crazybboy (Dreamstime), Darius Strazdas (Dreamstime), Igor Mojzes (Dreamstime), Irina Bekulova (Dreamstime), Jill Lang (Dreamstime), Lana Langlois (Dreamstime), Lukas Blazek (Dreamstime), Micaela Grace Sanna, Mike K. (Dreamstime), Photobunnyuk (Dreamstime), Raywoo (Dreamstime), Robert Byron (Dreamstime), Yulia Terentieva (Dreamstime), tea maeklong (Shutterstock)

Chapter 6: Alessandro Canova (Dreamstime), Alexkalashnikov (Dreamstime), Bblood (Dreamstime), Juliet Kim (Dreamstime), Jurra8 (Dreamstime), Konstantin Sutyagin (Dreamstime), Laindiapiaroa (Dreamstime), Micaela Grace Sanna, Natali Antoschenko (Dreamstime), Patrice Correia (Dreamstime), Stanislav Ríha (Dreamstime), Stef22 (Dreamstime), Tamara Bauer (Dreamstime)

Pages 69–72: Anthony Aneese Totah Jr (Dreamstime), Batuque (Dreamstime), Chan Yee Kee (Dreamstime), Chris Van Lennep (Dreamstime), Dndavis (Dreamstime), Ene (Dreamstime), George Mayer (Dreamstime), Hxdbzxy (Dreamstime), Ian Wilson (Dreamstime), Kristof Degreef (Dreamstime), Leonardo Viti (Shutterstock), Liumangtiger (Dreamstime), Ljupco (Dreamstime), Lucian Coman (Dreamstime), Micaela Grace Sanna, Mirko Dabi☐ (Dreamstime), Parthkumar Bhatt (Dreamstime), Rico Leffanta (Dreamstime), Rudmer Zwerver (Dreamstime), Steve Schowiak (Dreamstime), Subbotina (Dreamstime), Swisshippo (Dreamstime), Tamara Bauer (Dreamstime), Winzworks (Dreamstime)

CPSIA information can be obtained at www.ICGtesting.com
Printed in the USA
LVIW01n1211270117
522416LV00011B/162